Covering Rough Ground

KATE BRAID

Published by
Polestar Book Publishers,
P.O. Box 69382, Station K,
Vancouver, BC, V5K 4W6

Distributed by
Raincoast Book Distribution Ltd.,
112 East Third Avenue,
Vancouver, BC, V5T 1C8

Canadian Cataloguing in Publication Data

Braid, Kate
  Covering rough ground

  Poems.
  ISBN 0-919591-68-X

  I. Title.
PS8553.R34C6 1991   C811'.54   C91-091589-X
PR9199.3B72C6 1991

Published with the assistance of the Canada Council and B.C. Cultural Services Branch

To my mother and father,
Betty and Harry Braid

for giving me roots
and wings.

One does not always plant one's feet daintily
when one is covering rough ground.

—Emily Carr, *Journals*

CONTENTS

THE BIRTH OF BUILDINGS

SISTER IN THE BROTHERHOOD

WHERE SHE WANTS TO BE

WOMAN WHO KNOWS WOOD

THE BIRTH OF BUILDINGS

Concrete Fever

for Phil Vernon

Seven and one half yards of concrete
and every last pebble in place.
A certain kind of concrete steps
I'd never built before, and
six different patio slopes all having to run
with perfect symmetry
to that one post hole marker
of a drain pipe
and an architect antsy eagle eye for the least mistake
or merely visual flaw.

I worried, I cursed, I adjusted and nailed
and by six o'clock my steps are a grace
to behold, a joy to ascend
and the water from the hoses
of the concrete finisher
rolls sweetly down all those six slopes
and into that bull's-eye drain.
I love water!
I love concrete!
I love the work I did today!

Recipe for a Sidewalk

Pouring concrete is just like baking a cake.
The main difference is
that first you build the pans. Call them forms.
Think grand.
Mix the batter with a few simple ingredients:
      one shovel of sand
            one shovel of gravel
                  a pinch of cement.

Add water until it looks right.
Depends how you like it.
Can be mixed by hand or with a beater called
a Readi-Mix truck.
Pour into forms and smooth off.
Adjust the heat so it's not too cold,
not too hot. Protect from rain.
Let cook until tomorrow.
Remove the forms and walk on it.

There is one big difference from cakes.
This one will never disappear.
For the rest of your life your kids
will run on the same sidewalk, singing
My mom baked this!

In the Pink

It is a foul morning
when I wake up grumbling about
the ungodly hours of construction
then drop my thermos,
condemned to thirst all day
and late to work for cleaning up
the mess.
A lecture from the boss
who sticks me in a ditch
building an afterthought of a wall.
When the hammer slips
I am covered in muck, curse
the bad judgement that brought me here.

Then sun breaks through
and just for a second
on the slippery black rubber of my toe
is balanced the single petal
of a glorious fuscia bloom.
And suddenly this ditch
is the perfect setting
for pink.

Woman's Touch

Lunchtime, sitting on a lumber pile
in the middle of the construction site,
my eye fell
on Sam's 32 ounce hammer
with the 24 inch handle.

*How come all our tools
are longer than they are wide?*
I asked.

Silence.

Feeling reckless
with confidence because
that morning I'd cut
my first set of stairs
at a perfect fit, I pushed on.

*How come the hammer,
the saw, everything
except the tool belt looks like
you know what?*

Don't be so sensitive, Sam said.
How else could they be?
There was a chorus of grunts
in the bass mode.
Besides,
Sam was on firm ground now,
the circular saw is round.

Ed raised his head slowly.
The cirular saw was invented by a woman,
he said, and took a bite of salami.

He finished the meat then sat
quite still, contemplating his Oreo.
In 1810 in New England, he continued,
Sarah Babbitt's husband had a sawmill
where they cut the logs over a pit
with a man at each end of a huge hand saw.
She noticed they wasted half
their energy, for hand saws only cut
on the push. She had an idea.

Ed took a chocolate bite and chewed.
Even Sam was quiet.
She went into her kitchen,
fetched a tin dish and cut
teeth in it. Then she slipped it
onto the spindle of her spinning wheel,
fed a cedar shake into it
and the circular saw was born.

Ed folded his brown paper bag.
After a certain silence
Sam spat.
I knew there was something funny
about that saw, he said
and sulked off stomping sawdust.

Think Like a Weightlifter,
Think Like a Woman

First day on the job and the foreman orders
in a voice like a chainsaw,
Hoist those timbers
by hand to the second floor.
Crane's broken down.

I keep my mouth shut
with difficulty, knowing
how much a six by six timber
twelve feet long and fresh
from the Fraser River, knowing
how much it weighs.

Lorne, my partner, says nothing,
addresses the modest mountain of timbers
towering over our heads, smelling
sweetly nostalgic for forest.

Weighing in with the wood he faces,
with a belly like a great swelling bole,
he shakes off my motion to help and
bends as if to pick up a penny,
scoops up the timber and packs it, 50 feet,
to lean against the damp grey sides
of the concrete core.
When he doesn't look back,
it's my turn.

And now, because I need this job, and
because it's the first day and because
every eye is watching The Girl,
I bend my knees as the book says,
think like a weightlifter, take the beam
by its middle and order my body
to lift.

Reluctantly, the great tree, sweating pitch,
parts with its peers with a sucking sound,
and the beam and I sway to the designated spot,
I drop it. Repeat.

Alone, I carry beams to Lorne
who alone heaves them with the slightest grunt
to the labourer who bends from the second floor
with a hurry-up call,
Faster! Faster!

No. I will never be a carpenter, I think, *never
able to work like these men.* Then
Lorne falters.
Without thinking I reach up my two arms beside him
and push with all my might.
The beam flies to the second floor and mindless,
I turn to fetch him another.

Without a word
Lorne follows me back to the pile,
lifts one end and helps me
carry the next timber to the wall.
Without a word we both push it up,
continue this path together
find a rhythm, a pace
that feels more like dancing.

Lorne says, *You walk different.* Yes.
For on this day I am suddenly
much, much stronger, a woman with the strength
of two.

The Sacrament of Wood

Half priest, half peasant
framed
in the sweet smelling ribs
of her own created space,
a carpenter
can mend things, she can
build things but she can't
go inside
all this meaning.

Bending, she serves her creation
as fingers of roof throw
blueprints on her floor.
In this shelter she worships,
watches it
rise, irridescent with lightness
each day further above her,
bones rising, flesh
from her flesh,
its creaking breath of two by fours
awakened
by the kiss of her hammer.

Class Conscious

I put my hands on the table
right after you noticed the hammers
I wear for earrings.
An accidental gesture
     sort of.
The hands that wield a hammer
I wanted to show you
so there'd be no illusions
about me
       tough woman
       tough hands.
I didn't want you to get the wrong idea
about me
       looking so feminine in some parts.
What you see
my hands say for me
is what you get.

I put my hands on the table
tentative
proud   sort of
hoping you are one of the ones
who likes a working hand

and scared you're not.

Tool: Instrument for Getting a Grip on the World

it is the world outside my door which looks at times insane and exceedingly dangerous. it is my own inability that is so dangerous. the worst is that we (that we again) have made it so. no, the worst is, we had no say in how it was made .... perhaps that explains why our writing, which we also live inside of, is different from men's, and not a tool, not a "pure instrument for getting a grip on the world."

— Daphne Marlatt, *Ana Historic*

1. Hammer

Hammer, you are number one/androgyne.
Don't tell
how I love your shape, long
like a man,
the ridges in your sides rubbed smooth
like a woman
by my hand.

Let me hold you close
to the callus,
guide your energy, flow of
head to nail, to wood, to waler and stud,
all of my power to drive
further
in to the places I love
the best, the wood.
Drive it
home, my man   power
woman power
mine. Yes!

2. Saw

Saw is the sensitive one
unforgiving, impatient with her own
power so be careful.

Always a talker, she chants or whines
depending on how
you treat her.
She's never, ever afraid so know
that her teeth can bite
rough stuff
on wood, or flesh.

Take her straight
to the wood, no fooling around.
She loves to eat, use her teeth
to nibble on chamfer
or tear up the garden posts, an Amazon
witch in the magic of divide and create.
Some call her aggressive but
she

is the Zen tool, needs a clear hand
draw her straight
to the heart
of fir and cedar and pine.
If you force her
she'll scream.
Use your ears, your ears to know
how a carpenter loves her saw.

3. Nail Puller

Oh this is a lovely tool, ticklish
with laughter. When those nails are
stuck or bend in the wind or
hiding, we laugh
knowing nail puller is close in our belts.
So easy, she is
a trick of the hand, a tap
of the hammer. Nails
sing with the ease of it all
come out
when called. The nail puller is
irresistible.

4. Tool Belt

Pockets like a mouth, giving kisses,
mother-like
she is
        home for the family,
filling every need
for pencils and nails,
chaulk line and wrench.

Tool belt cares for me, hugs
my hips with arms
that adjust to anything,
tender and tough,
holds everything
together.

5. Tape Measure

is tough, absolutely unforgiving
laying down a hard line of
order! Five six seven
no fooling, she's
pitting the force of her small black
fingers
against chaos.

She's a suck-your-cheeks-in
straight ahead lady, rolling
out figures like buns on bake day.
Only a click to her red-shoed feet
can make her pause
in gobbling up all that
consequence.

6. Framing Square

is too stiff for words.
Has *no*
sense of humour.
Ever. Always
sees things
in proportion.

This is the voice of reason.
How else
could roofs and angles flow
from all that
straight-line
lumber?

Small arm to large arm,
rise to run,
don't talk
when the square is framing.
She's thinking, she's
thinking, she's putting the world
in proportion
building castles in the air.

"Always keep your tools in shape."

– Carpenter's manual

I ask my body now,
pump my breasts for information.
Is my belly happy today?
Does the skin tingle?
Is my joy aware of itself?
Is there a sort of exhuberance
underneath it all, a foundation
of ebb and flow
and does the moontide sing in my veins?

Ph.D. in Construction

Lorne is a good carpenter,
catches the foreman's mistakes,
knows what's coming next.
One day he finds out
that I have a university degree.

We stop work for a moment while he
pulls out the blue bandana he stores
like a good luck token
in his left back pocket.
As he rubs the back of his neck
Lorne eyes the wall we are building
and approves.

I am a professional, he announces.
I've built office towers, pulp mills, dams.
Spent four years studying,
apprentice to a carpenter, same
as your Bachelor of Science
and twenty-six more
perfecting my hand.
You could say I have
a Ph.D. in construction.

I am only a third year apprentice.
For the rest of the job I call him
Doctor Lorne.

Metamorphosis

Lumber yard. Tool rental. Tarpaulin shop.
These are the clubhouses of the working men
where they talk real loud,
show posters of naked women,
bump tattoos.

All morning I sneak on kitten's feet
from one post to the other,
purring
so as not to offend
the elected.

But where are the clubhouses of the women?
Where can a carpenter put up her boots
slam her hardhat to the counter
and roar
like a lion in heat?

The Little Poem

Size is a big thing in construction.
Everything is measured and found wanting—
tools, materials, people.

> *How big is your hammer?*
> *Is that all?*
> *Don't you have anything heavier?*
> *Is that the best you can do?*

After a while I wonder,
couldn't we do as well with smaller parts,
more skill?
Imagine building a tower
with teeny weeny hammers
and a big heart?
There'd be less to throw away
and less to clean.

An itsy bitsy tower would linger near the ground,
smell the daisies.
We'd cut less trees and haul less rock.
Smaller hands,
a woman's perhaps,
could build this very well.
Think how far moonlight could travel
over such a delicate space.

We would have to balance
everything.
With less to make, less to borrow, less to buy
we might spend more time
thinking of little,
dreaming dreams
small enough to put our arms around.

SISTER IN THE BROTHERHOOD

Sister in the United Brotherhood of Carpenters & Joiners of America

I have to take away
all the parts that are
woman of me,
have to not care.
It's a skill
I learn from the men's
white granite confidence.
They smile as I leave.
Be tough! They say it
kindly

> *women can't*
> *take it you have*
> *to be hard*
> *like nails, ha ha*
> *look at me*

The men own the words
so far.
I learn this language
cold, hide
behind concrete
learn to love
that it is soft
and hard at once.
It's not you, they say

> *you're much too sensitive*
> *I only said Don't*
> *call me Person*
> *you joined*
> *the Brotherhood we're*
> *in this together*
> *it was mine*
> *first*

It doesn't really hurt
if I take apart my little
soft self, put my Woman
in a basket
send her away to be
reclaimed
someday
if I'm not lost forever
by then
it's just
'til this battle's won only
it might take a little
longer

> *you can't be pushy, can't*
> *rush some things one day*
> *you'll understand*
> *everything*
> *you won't feel a thing*
> *trust me*

First Woman

Hidden,
an identity of thistles,
I reveal my goals in glimpses,
am granted part-time acceptance
only when no one is looking.

Shielded,
they huddle close
to each other, talking
shop, chanting
confirmation of every male
rite. Male-clad, afraid, as if

I hide some terrible weapon
of woman's knowing,
as if we fight some war
only one of us can remember.

Brothers

We have worked together
eight hours every day,
five days every week,
four weeks every month,
for three months now.
Closer than a marriage almost
in the intensity of our days,
the joy in our joint production.

We have fought for each other
and refused to be separated
by other carpenters
or a foreman's whim
and yesterday they said
there will be layoffs next week.

Don't get excited, you said
when the tears sprang to my eyes.

Don't get excited, you have said before.
It is our joke of the past three months
and now I understand
that *excited* means *emotional.*
I'm not allowed to care on this job
yet you love me because I speak the unspoken.
I cry the tears for us all.

Summer Rites

All right you guys, you win!
Here's one more
hell of a hot day and you all
have bare chests and
once too often you've asked
that stunningly witty question,
When will you *take off* your *T-shirt, Kate?*

So here I go! Open your eyes and look!
No T-shirt now, just me
and my skin feels great
in the cool tingle of breeze
at last drying sweat.
Already I feel brown all over.
Why haven't I done this
                    sooner?

What?
It embarrasses you to see
my biceps flash
when I swing this hammer?
You never knew it was muscle
                    beneath all these curves?

You want what?
No brother. When the shirt comes off
it's off.
You'll simply have
to lower your eyes
when the woman walks by.

"Girl" on the Crew

The boys flap heavy leather aprons at me
like housewives scaring crows
from the clean back wash.
     Some aprons.   Some wash.
They think if the leather is tough enough
if the hammer handle piercing it is long enough
I will be overcome with primordial dread
or longing.

They chant construction curses at me:
   Lay 'er down! Erect those studs!
and are alarmed when I learn the words.
They build finely tuned traps, give orders I cannot fill
then puzzle when a few of their own
give me pass words.

I learn the signs of entry,
dropping my hammer into its familiar mouth
as my apron whispers *O-o-o-h Welcome!*

I point my finger and corner posts spring into place
shivering themselves into fertile earth at my command.
The surveyors have never seen such accuracy.

I bite off nails with my teeth
shorten boards with a wave of my hand
pierce them through the dark brown love knots.
They gasp.

I squat and the flood of my urine digs
whole drainage systems in an instant.
The boys park their backhoes, call their friends
to come see for themselves or they'd never believe it.

The hairs of my head turn to steel and join boards
tongue-in-groove
like lovers along dark lanes.
Drywall is rustling under cover
eager to slip over the studs at my desire.

When I tire, my breasts grow two cherry trees
that depart my chest
and offer me shade, cool juices
while the others suck bitter beans.

At the end of the day the boys are exhausted
from watching.
They fall at my feet and beg for a body like mine.
I am too busy dancing to notice.

Contradictions

Going back to work this time
I had almost forgotten how easily
some men fall in love
with a woman who bridges the gap,
who teases their manhood
at its root   at work,
who shakes it a little
with that style of feminine
that swings a mean hammer.

I had almost forgotten
the moment of light in their eyes
when they hear themselves say,
I liked working with you today.
And the confusion
later
when they stumble
over this new knowledge.

I had almost forgotten the time
when I complained my hands
were like sandpaper
and Charlie laughed,
You're supposed to say
they're getting nicely into shape.
Or the time he moved a wall
three quarters of an inch
with two spikes and a 28 ounce hammer and said,
Carpenters are nice people because
the material we work with
is so forgiving.

I had almost forgotten the contradictions,
so onion sweet
they make my eyes water.

Something Aching

At coffee break the electrician is celebrating
forty-eight years in his trade.
We press him to tell how he started
in Denmark, at age 14.
Instead he talks of the war.
*I joined the underground when I was still
apprentice,* he begins
his voice fading to memory.

*Coming back from one expedition
we were too many for the van
so two of us took the truck.
The Nazis stopped the van and all of my friends
were tortured.*

*By age 17 I had killed the Nazi
who pulled the fingernails
of a friend
who refused to talk.*

He puts down his coffee.
*What I learned from that
is you do not forget.
Twenty years later when I saw*
The Sound of Music
*where the Nazis invade Austria
I shook so badly
I had to leave the theatre.*

*Also I learned
you must always be vigilant,
that the greatest danger
is from within.*
He stands, as if to return to work
or to relieve the pain
of something aching.
His voice is thick with effort.
*The Nazi I killed was no German
but a fellow Dane.*

Great Moments in Construction

1. The Carpenter

for Jacqueline Frewin

This too
            is camaraderie
to sit at midnight with the other woman
carpenter. We decided together
to kick the drywallers off the job
for gross incompetence
and have finished their work
in time for tomorrow's deadline.

Now we can sit
exhausted by a 16 hour day
drinking peppermint tea and laughing
over how we would act
if *we* had been stoned on this job.

I would have measured the space between nails,
you said and we giggled
                              giddy with fatigue then
sat silent by the beam of a trouble light
admiring our work
proud of what we'd done,
proud
            we'd done it together.

2. The Plumber

The plumber gives excellent service.
We all are impressed by how early
he gets to the job, how late
he stays. We tell him
Ease off but he insists
he doesn't mind working Saturday
again.

Later we find the note
with flowers
for the nanny in the basement suite
signed *Love,*
The Plumber.

3. The Concrete Finisher

The pit floor in the elevator shaft
on 14th Avenue is filling with water.
Nobody knows exactly what to do
but there has been no lack of suggestions.
Maybe it's the joins, someone says.
Finish the drain tile first, adds another.

The three of us who built it,
two carpenters and a concrete finisher
stand close, our arms swung vine-like
around fragrant lumber, hanging
over the black, mouldy smell
of elevator turned sump.

Vern, the concrete finisher,
pokes with a stick and we all stare dumbly
at the shocking levels of water revealed
by the wet wood, luminous
in the near dark.

Vern drops his head as if to listen
to the tiny tinkle of water.
I think, he says
in an accent rich with the dark florals
of the Caribbean,
*You can't do a damn thing 'til you figure out
where this water coming from.*
And we hang like three flowers,
two pinks and a chocolate brown
waiting for the answer to rise up
from the five o'clock depths of a Friday afternoon
at the elevator shaft.

4. The Salesman

The salesman from the window company
is short
        and round.
His name is Bill and he mops his forehead
frequently,
sees nothing wrong with plastic arches
in a solid wood door
but is happy to discuss it
        at length.

Sometimes we women keep working, the carpenter
the contractor and the apprentice.
Then Bill talks
        a lot.
Tells us about cheap drinks
in Blaine. One day he comes right out
and asks the contractor to come
for a beer.
She is in a ditch at the time
laying drain tile, wading
        in mud.

Bill goes to the public library,
arrives one day waving a sheet
of paper, hot
off the copy machine.
I looked up your company name,
ZENOBIA, he says
and shows the picture of an Amazon queen
looking so like the woman in front of him
        she might have been her mother.

He reads bits of the story aloud
and we all stop work to listen, hear his voice
rise in alarm
when it comes to the part
where Zenobia kills off her husband.
The contractor looks over his shoulder.

Yes, she says. *That was before*
divorce, and goes back
        to her work.

5. The Drywaller

The drywaller is a Buddhist.
When the foreman calls him for work
he can't come to the phone because
      he's chanting.

The drywaller is working on
his spiritual development
on levels far different from the daily ones
of cut and lift and nail
that he practices
all day
      every week
          all year,
the work of his body opposed
to the work of his soul.

The drywaller announced that he marches
to a different drummer.
Perhaps that explains
the three hour lunches
from which he returns, sort of,
in a way suggestive of something
      beer, perhaps,
the work of his body
opposed
to the work of his soul.

Crucified

for Bishop Remi de Roo

You say if Jesus returned
we would know him
by his hands.

You could say that about
any carpenter,
the seams and calluses
of our palms marking us

permanently
as people of the outdoors
stroking rough wood
everyday in every weather.

A simple religion of labour
our crucifixion would be
      to make us stop,
our resurrection
      the chance to work again.

General Strike, 1987

See this sign? *In Protest* it says
but it says more, things
you won't see printed here
no matter how hard you strain
those eyes.

It says I'm fed up with all this
farting around.
I can't talk pretty like some
but I know that I vote
for every damned thing
in my union. Now tell me
the last time the boss
asked my opinion on the foreman's salary
or how fast the green chain moves,
though nobody knows better than me
what could make that place hum
for the better of all of us.

I give 'em my blood and my muscle
for eight hours of the day and still
they say when I work and "if" and
when I take a break and "if" and whether
they'll give me earmuffs for the job or
if I got to buy my own, though
you go deaf fast without 'em
and some days
it's a half hour overtime, no extra pay,
'cause the boss has a rush on, no care
that I'm the one got to pick up the kids
'cause the wife works afternoons.

So when they said I have too much power
I damn split a gut laughing, 'til
they told me I didn't have a job no more
lest I work for less.
If this is too much power then
what do I make of Timothy Eaton or Conrad Black
who don't seem too worried about the next
mortgage payment or if they can send their eldest
to a better school 'cause teacher says
she's bright.

Me and the people like me,
we built this province, board by board
and we built it good
and if this government says
I'm a traitor for asking
for a steady job or the right to question
what they did to make my work life worse
then I'm on the march. See this sign? It says
I'm fed up
with all this farting around.

Union Love Poem: For Local 452

We meet in small back rooms
and union halls,
me the only woman
with these plain brown men.

We argue for hours
over strategy, laughing
when things threaten
to become personal, dig in
for another round.
We are planning our future.

John leans forward,
red plaid jacket brushing mine
and points to the sawdust on my knees.
Bet you put that there on purpose.
I smile. He knows
I spent this day renovating.
Eau de sawdust, Bill whispers
from the other side.

When the meeting is adjourned
we push back chairs,
trade jokes and news.
First, *Are you working?* Then, *Where?*
It is banter but underneath it
is the bedrock certainty
that these men, carpenters all,
would be pillars to hold to
should any of us fall
on a job, in a strike, on a picket line.

Here, tonight, I know the meaning
of camaraderie and I am in love
with a roomful of brothers.

Union Welders: Overtime

for Sandy Shreve

My brothers are building a dome
of crazed bars jutting
stiff into Expo air.

I watch them at night
hundreds of feet off the ground
magnificently poised
up where the air is clear.
As they work they are stars to me
shooting novas as they strike their arcs,
set welding rods
and build.

That's not welders, my son explains
sixteen and wise.
Those are lights, set to flash.
Construction is finished,
done.

That night it is joyless to me.
I see builders no more,
just the built
ugly attempt
to mimic heaven.

Carpenter

everyone has scars . . .

                    Michael Ondaatje

This is who I am
this is what I do
and these are the scars I bear:

thick fingers of muscle, scar tissue
over old cuts from the utility knife,
chisels that missed,
nails that didn't

one finger gimped by a hammer that fell
too soon, finger nails
that out of politeness
should never be outlined again
in red and hands that in your wildest
imaginings you could not call
soft again

a back that aches regardless of
stretches each morning
and a steady cough
from the allergy I bear
to wood dust.

Deeper still I show
a tendency to talk to my wood.
Some call it madness, others
nod. They've seen it before
in a pride that loves to say

I built that
and a love a mile wide
for fellow carpenters because
I know their secrets,
our shared passion for wood
no matter what.

These Hips

Some hips are made for bearing
children, built like stools
square and easy, right
for the passage of birth.

Others are built like mine.
A child's head might never pass
but load me up with two-by-fours
and watch me
bear.

When the men carry sacks of concrete
they hold them high, like boys.
I bear mine low, like a girl
on small, strong hips
built for the birth
of buildings.

WHERE SHE WANTS TO BE

The Birth: October 19, 1988

When Pam grows tired
I help hold her legs
for the baby to come,
a V for victory
for hours.

The nurse says push
to the count of ten
and I count with her, *Four, five, six*
and beyond to *Thirteen*, magic,
the number of the women.

The nurse, the doctor, the husband,
Pam and Vicky and I all
wait.
The room is a cave full of six silences
and my voice
counting.

As each pain passes Pam opens her eyes,
her face an open box of questions.
We're still here, I say
then the spasm comes
and her face closes slowly, like a train
chuffing goodbye, a bird
flying south to mysteries.

Eleven, twelve, then she's gone,
the lonely numbers her only baggage
'til all of us tire, the train slows but now
Don't stop!

 And the babe is a vein of opals,
a splendid view through the mist
of her skin, a glimpse
of wet brown curls, the most perfect
scenery.

Thirteen, yes!
and the baby, yes! is blue
the sky, the sky, *Suction!*
Push!
and she's here, she's here
the destination and
the delivered.
Denika is
born.

In Honour of Sasha

Tonight I am reading a book about surviving
in Auschwitz and yesterday I helped Jude
deliver her baby after 48 hours of labour and now
I am thinking about pain, about

how mundane it is
for some people
like mothers, like Jude.
How she laboured
(the rest of us know nothing
about hard work) and she pushed
for all those single hours
with sometimes a drug but mostly
not and how

after 48 hours of her body cut
and punctured from inside and out she had
a baby, great, a girl
and five minutes later
looking rested and glorious
with Sasha on her chest, this woman
who hadn't eaten or slept in two days
murmured, *Wouldn't it be nice*
to have a sister or brother for Sasha,

and that's when I thought about Auschwitz
and the ones who were stripped naked, sick,
made to wait in the cold for days and given
no water when they needed the doctor
and one of those patients delivered
a book out of all that, and then another

and I wondered at how we forget what we need to
and remember what we want to and how
human spirit itself is the miracle, like
a rosy dawn that keeps rising, regardless
of Holocaust or everyday agony, how people

always find the seed that brings a flower,
a new creature from all that and I guess that's why
I'm alive too. To keep it going.
To toast that dawn, that book,
that baby. To say, Me too.
Le chaim! To life!

Sisters to Mothers

When you were pregnant
my body, like the sister string
on a finely tuned harp, vibrated
with needing a baby too.

Then, your labour was my labour
and now your womb is empty
and the crib is full
I am exhausted
by your effort,
thrilled by your daughter,
and the thing is done.

Your shadow, your clone,
when you bend to kiss her
my body dips and my lips
feel silk.
Now I know what men feel
when they say, *"We"*
have a baby.

Step Son

for Kevin Steeves

For someone who never had a baby
I'm not doing too bad
sitting here in a high school auditiorium just like
a real parent,
trying not to be too obvious when I wave back at
the sort of subtle flourishes of the first clarinet.
Positively dashing, this child not-of-my-body,
born of seven years of my care.
My heart dances with delight and even
gratitude, me who was always too impatient
to wait for a baby to grow. Now look at me,
blessed with a fifteen year old man
who bends over from six feet of solicitude
and honours me with the question asked only of friends,
How's it goin', dude?

Amelia Gwendolyn, 1886 – 1982

Some of my ancestors were women,
lived right
alongside their men
and never got noticed
except to be married
                    commended
for their endurance
                    invisibly.

Some of my ancestors
rocked the boat
along with the cradle and sang
warrior songs with lust in their eyes
caught food and killed it and ate
and thanked the goddess.
Carried on

bore babies, some of my ancestors did,
raised bees, mowed hay
and all along they were heras
that nobody noticed,
forgotten,
except for the odd
line in Amelia's Bible, the odd
word like a seed
waiting

        for water.

Strong Arms, Strong Heart: 1920

Four children I have
and a farm. No man.

A yard full of dust
a heart full of wheat

and a Bible I wear
like a breastplate
of salvation.

At twenty I came
from Dublin
with a dowry of quilts
and lace, a history
of selling fine hats.

The house was as he said,
still creaking fresh
and smelling of honey
in the middle of a Prairie sea,
no woman for miles.

Rich in children,
I built a world
out of soap and water
ashes and lye
my own strong arms
strong heart.

When the man died
I worked harder. Sent the boys to school.
The girls
carried milk, piled hay, ran horses,
cooked for the hired men at harvest.

When I die, the boys
will take the farm. The girls
will marry. It is
God's will, it is
what I have lived for.

> Four children I have
> and a farm. No man.
>
> A yard full of dust
> a heart full of wheat
>
> and a Bible I wear
> like a breastplate
> of salvation.

Auntie

for Kathleen Coates and Kelly Pryde

In dreams I draw my finger
over your dusty welding rods
forbidden since the war
when they said married women
can't do men's work
anymore,
should be home minding babies,
sewing smocks for new citizens.
A woman's place, you always said,
was where she wants to be.
That was the war we all lost

that time.

Nanaimo Crossing

The ferry's wake is a deep row
gouged in the field of ocean,
mountains benign and distant.
They will only care
    rustling themselves into scenic shadows
if Tony Onley agrees to paint.
Tourists are largely neglectful
more concerned with their lovers
or the Nanaimo Free Press.

The top button of my yellow blouse
keeps slipping open
and the pimply teen across my table
has noticed.
I entertain a fantasy before I leave
to sit at the stern.

I crave the chocolate bar
of the four year old beside me,
stare hard
hoping she will read my mind
or drop a piece.
I try thought control,
consider violence.
I know these thoughts are not
Correct
so I close my eyes.
Now no one can find me.

The man in front of me
has bullet holes in the back of his vest.
I wonder if he was in it at the time
or if one of the green canadian cadets
in neat rows around him
had anything to do with it.

It seems every baby on the Lower Mainland
has come along for this ride.
Perhaps it is Baby Spring Break.
A pink one hits the dust and screams
baby revenge.
We all feel guilty and glare at the mother.

A child, perhaps three
asks the woman wielding the vacuum,
Are you the captain?
No, she replies, *but I could use the promotion.*

To my left a young boy puts arms
around his father's neck.
They nuzzle with kisses.
Where have I been all my life
that men are so tender.
I fall in love with the father.

This affair is ended
by the doorbell that introduces
the recorded voice that announces
Nanaimo.

The passengers board their bus,
newspapers folded and stowed
according to instructions.
I am in my vehicle when the ferry docks.
By law in BC you must use
your seatbelt.
All others use
the overhead walkway
on the Promenade Deck.

Woman Bush Pilot: 1

What does it take?
Remember when we talked about
what they say, that
women can't fly this plane
          (crude jokes about Beavers)
and I told you the secret, that
it doesn't take a man
to push a button marked
                              Power!

But they keep talking and
after a while
I start to wonder
(the doubt like rust)
maybe I *can't*
fly.

The time I helped John load the plane
and he said
slow down but I loaded double I was
going to show them until
my left arm slipped
and the bucket pulled my arm down hard
so I hit my jaw on the step
said nothing, kept loading
John flew away and still I said nothing
for one more month. The jaw
was broken. What
does it take?

Woman Bush Pilot: 2

Defying the evidence of eyes
they lied, insisted
women can't fly.
But I kept flying, carrying
all that weight,
overcoming
mountains
ill will
trailing like exhaust.
The plane was shrouded with it.

They said one woman alone
can't, I didn't know
I too   was caught
until that day
even the lake
was distorted
and I trusted the surface,
pushed the nose down
to kiss its reflection under
water, too soon
another
lie.

Woman Bush Pilot: 3

Don't kid yourself
I am
shattered glass
I am
putting the pieces back together.
The accident was
my fault
I am responsible. The water was glass
I could only see my reflection
they said I couldn't   but
a pilot is   of course   I take
full responsibility

apart from my jaw outside and hurt
on the inside
there were no other injuries
to me
but I am responsible
for the others

I thought I would go crazy.

Women as far away as Telegraph Creek
they write
we don't know what to say but
   we love you.

When we hit I was thrown out
through the space where the windshield
used to be
and as soon as I landed
I knew
I was the only one alive and I thought
I only have to take a deep breath
it will all be over but   I didn't
I kept going under
I can't swim you know but
somehow I came up
for the rescue

don't laugh but
all my life I have tested myself
I ask, What is the worst that could happen?
and the worst was that I would crash
and kill somebody and me
alive

I ask myself   Why am I alive?

that night another pilot visited me
in the clinic
only small talk but afterward
I thought he'd never know how much it meant
he looked me straight in the eye.
You'd do the same for me, he said.

I am a piece of glass
shattered and now
I have to put together the pieces
and I will
I will put together   everything
but

I could have just died.

The day after the crash
they wired shut my jaw
and after two weeks I could have screamed
I took the pliers and pulled out the strands
all the little bits   that were muzzling me

It's the women mostly
they keep me from going crazy.
One woman widowed twice
came to my house and said
I forgive you   and
when you forgive yourself
you will be whole

the women are the strongest
I would have gone crazy
they are a ray of light and
don't kid yourself

I will
put together
all
the pieces.

Woman Bush Pilot: 4

for Theresa Bond

You mourned and were crazy
especially when your husband died
within months of the crash
but you did it then
just as you promised,
you found a new man
(or he found you)
someone who cheered for your side
for a change,
and you began again
putting it all together.

The neighbours sniffed
and disapproved and wouldn't
speak to That Man in your house
but he made you laugh
and you started eating again.
(*You even got tits,* he said.)

When I saw the pictures of you
one year later
I didn't recognize you
laughing and happy
in China.

They promised the two of you
a job together
training staff
for a Western style hotel.
My energy, your brains, he said.
Just three months back home
to clear up loose ends, time
to get married, then back
to China for two years
with all the pieces
together again.
It could have been
perfect.

Woman Bush Pilot: 5

Sister, it makes me grieve, how
the newspapers gave the barest account.
They always treated you barely.
But they had time to say
*The same woman pilot
of the plane that crashed,
killing five* and listed
all your previous accidents, mistakes.
This was meant to explain everything.

It makes me want to cry, how
they got you in the end. Dead
by some other pilot's hand.
They didn't specify, *Male pilot
makes error, kills self
and two others, a woman
and a five year old child.*

It makes me want to scream, how
they didn't list his previous accidents,
let the man rest in peace
something they don't dare let you
lest some other woman take up the challenge,
press the right buttons
without a single thing between her legs
except the ordinary
courage, every woman's
                              power.
It makes me want
to fly.

Pass the Pain

for Eleanor Knight

My muscles grow taut from physical work
and what do they learn
from all this clenching?
To send my hands numb every morning,
a twist of pain in my back,
the strain
of an eternally aching shoulder.

I lay this imbalanced body, an offering
on the masseuse's table.
Her hands and shoulders, strong
like mine, work
to lift the knots of muscle brittle with armour.

But where does the hurt go as it seeps
from my skin into hers?
What pains of mine does she carry home
at night?
Who takes her tired shoulders
after a day of blessing the rest of us,
and gives her ease?
Where does this long cycle of aching
end?

The Taste of Pink

Last month with hundreds of men
in that one room
I hardly noticed the tightness of their flat hard chests
muscled smooth beneath plaid shirts,
low voices whose rumble I now accept
as normal.

So sitting with one hundred women
I am culture shocked amid
one hundred pairs of breasts
rolling round and warm over these flat hard eyes,
dazzled by cotton and silk cascading off
round hills of hips,
colours so strong they pulse.
My ears feel the beat,
rich bass and treble of purple and red
and my tongue feels thick
with the taste of pink.

The Other Side

A building crew of strong women
aggressively female,
raging and glorious dykes

bear resemblance that would shock them
so like all the crews
of my construction life
of strong men
aggressively male.

Each holds an anger to the
Other that hammers down
naked rage.

What cuts have we given each other?
What violence afflicted,
that furies spill so hard?

And what terrible mystery
when men and women who have never met
declare a mutual war?

Thieves Bay

I drive you to the ferry after not enough said
and you kiss me, still silent.
You are leaving with something of mine.

Later, I walk in the fog for hours.

Only the rocks are clear, and the water
and the ducks, calling to each other
constantly, keeping in touch.

The Relationship

Listening to the news I hear that
a polar bear crawled onto the ice and ate
one of the four dogs.   I wondered
how much blood. Was it like
the time we fought, the first time
I hit you, horrified to see the blood
drain from your face.   You said
it was all right   turned from me
your back like an ice floe I clung to
shaking with cold.

The bear ate the second dog
just as I screamed
knowing my heart would burst
that time you left and wouldn't come back
all night   there was only the sound of my bones
being sucked dry, knowing
what was coming
next

the bear ate the third dog and police fired
a warning shot   that missed, like the time
you tried to hit me but I blocked
with my arm and we stared
into each other's eyes
across frozen waste   it wasn't even hate
it was   knowing

and then the police shot the bear.

Song of Myself as Creator

When I was in exile I had no home.
Even the fishes have water
and birds have air. Alone I wandered until
one stick fell into my hand and in my sorrow

I beat on it and thus created two.
I crossed these two and bound them
with my hair and here is a door through which

I enter. Over my head trees whisper, lend me
their limbs, shelter summer green.
I invite the birds for song
yellow, call on the colour of crystals

and I have a home whose root
is as deep as the spruce with a softness
like breath. Now my limbs

fill with a power unquenchable
and my eyes burn with the strength
of my desire and the strength of my hands
and all who know it dream to enter here.

The women especially, they make a humming sound
like the humming at the bottom of the ocean.
They are humming mauve, burgundy, purple and red.
It is the start of everything over again,
A chorus like ocean. It sounds home, it says home
I am here.

WOMAN WHO KNOWS WOOD

A History of My Meetings with Emily Carr

1. National Gallery, Ottawa

In the first paintings
little yellow sunshine people play about the base
of polite totem poles,
senses intact.
But as the years roll by
people are left behind entirely
forgotten for the thick wet slicks
of light and darkness.

I was happy enough. You had become
a carver of space and colour, modelled
after the poles you loved but now
as I turn to the large wall,
suddenly this. Shocked
at the licentiousness of greens
I grow flustered, forget to look for a title.
Order slips while
Eros grows up my legs and my nipples crackle
under the promise of bark.

Surely this picture should be hidden by draperies?
Emily, such a tree from you, sixty years old
and eccentric as all get out
with your monkey and dogs
promenading on Government Street.
A Victorian woman you, and yet
these paintings show no shame, as if
you wouldn't even shriek when another pole
huge, dark, male
entered your canvas, straining
to meet with the sky.

It gets worse on the next wall
and I am afraid to meet the eye
of other tourists, afraid
they will see the lust carved here.
I fall into a chair for relief.
Give me a cool Harris, someone,
a merely obsessive Michael Snow!

Emily, you! Old and fat and dare to flaunt
such spirit! Is this why Lawren Harris
encouraged you from a distance? Surely he
licked his lips when another of those
cedar heavy boxes arrived, breathing
musk and dark while
his own canvases lay frozen in ice?
It must have been you, stroked
his Arctic blues into balance,
the passion of the west's romance for a perfect
Canadian businessman.

2. British Columbia Forest

Emily, I could taste you,
the salad of your palette,
bitter chocolate of tree trunks
and totem poles climbing into skies drenched
with green and blue and light.

And down below,
when green ran like smoke through the forest,
ripe with the smell of feasts coming,
what did you do then
on your little camp stool, in your caravan,
with only the poles and the trees and the paint?

3. Top of Small Trees, Lower Branches of Large One

It is marked, innocently enough
by a year
circa 1929/30 it says, but really
it is the sign
of where it all began.
The beginning of the end,
you wise woman, you
were here
when you first looked up
above the top of the small trees
to the lower branches of a large one.

You know what they say
to us women   Never
raise your eyes.
What you see
may haunt you. Absolutely
correct. And haunt the rest
of us through you
ever after.

Top of Small Trees, Lower
Branches of Large One
must be where you shifted, lifted
those eyes, began crawling upward
one painful branch
at a time, let
angels and devils loose
and made us see
trees with lips, with lives.
It is a terrible secret you tell.

4. Pines in May

Dancing.
Did you ever see a tree
dancing? She did.
Young ones at the front,
adolescents behind
and a mother over all
towering out of sight.
But the great
grandmother of everything
is sky.

Whenever she gives us sky
it is a blue gift of grace
making all the rest possible.

Pine trees frisking in great
spirals whose goal is always
upward.
Pine trees dancing in May,
a private party
and you one of the few
who could read the invitation.
There will be dancing,
it would say
written on cedar and fir and pine
in an envelope of deep black dirt.

5. Wood Interior 1909

There it is, earlier still.
Such a naive picture,
with all the parts we are
supposed to recognize as
bark   leaves   branches
green in its place.
You felt it like that then.

But even this early
your spirit stares
and sees what is between the trees
joining them.
It is a space
any carpenter would understand.
It is the reason we build things.
Looks like air to some,
fresh breeze, a touch of chill
or fog.
It is the spirit of the tree.

Now I know who you are.
Another woman who knows wood.

A portion of this collection has previously appeared in
*Canadian Dimension, Contemporary Verse 2, Don't Quit Yr
Day -Job, Fireweed, Malahat Review, Our Times, Room of
One's Own, This Magazine,* and *Tradeswomen,* as well as in
*East of Main, More Than Our Jobs (Pulp Press), Paperwork
(Harbour Press),* and *If I Had A Hammer (Papier Mache).*

Author photo by John Steeves
Cover photograph by Beth Beeson
Cover design by Jim Brennan
Typeset by The Vancouver Desktop Publishing Centre
Printed in Canada by Gagne Printing

Printed on paper
containing over 50%
recycled paper including
5% post-consumer fibre.

Printed in Canada